Stardust Media

University of Massachusetts Press

AMHERST AND BOSTON

STARDUST MEDIA

CHRISTINA
PUGH

Copyright © 2020 by University of Massachusetts Press
All rights reserved
Printed in the United States of America
ISBN 978-1-62534-511-0 (paper)

Designed by Deste Roosa
Set in Adobe Caslon Pro
Printed and bound by Maple Press, Inc.

Cover design by Deste Roosa
Cover art by James Abbott McNeil Whistler, *Nocturne in Black and Gold, the Falling Rocket,*
1875, oil on Panel. Detroit Institute of Arts, Gift of Dexter M. Ferry Jr.

Library of Congress Cataloging-in-Publication Data
Names: Pugh, Christina, author.
Title: Stardust media / Christina Pugh.
Description: Amherst : University of Massachusetts Press, [2020] |
Identifiers: LCCN 2019044411 | ISBN 9781625345110 (paperback) | ISBN
  9781613767603 (ebook) | ISBN 9781613767610 (ebook)
Subjects: LCGFT: Poetry.
Classification: LCC PS3616.U35 S73 2020 | DDC 811/.6—dc23
LC record available at https://lccn.loc.gov/2019044411

British Library Cataloguing-in-Publication Data
A catalog record for this book is available from the British Library

To my mother, and in memory of my father

CONTENTS

ACKNOWLEDGMENTS

Grateful acknowledgment is made to the editors of the following publications, in which some of these poems have appeared:

The Atlantic: "Toll"

The Eloquent Poem Anthology (Persea Books, ed. Elise Paschen): "Shirt Noise"

Fifth Wednesday: "Alba," "Hot or Cool Media," "*Linden*," "Now Whither for Brighter Colors?"

Hotel Amerika: "Heads Up," "I Don't Know How to Make a Website," "Portofino"

Ocean State Review: "With a Song"

Ploughshares: "The Social Fabric"

Plume: "But the Avant-Garde"

Plume Anthology of Poetry 6 (MadHat Press, ed. Daniel Lawless): "Scribble"

Plume Poetry 8 (Canisy Press, ed. Daniel Lawless): "The Close-Up"

Terrain.org: "Integrity," "Origins of the Collection," "Voice Road"

Yale Review: "Flirt," "The Staircase"

I am grateful to the John Simon Guggenheim Memorial Foundation for a fellowship that supported the completion of this book. My sincere thanks also to the Bogliasco Foundation and to the Virginia Center for the Creative Arts for residencies that provided both the solitude and the conversations that were integral to the book's development. My gratitude to Phillis Levin and Linda Bierds for their support and encouragement of this work; and to Lisa Petrie, Jason Roush, and Harriet Melrose for their sustaining friendship. Many thanks to Dara Wier, Arda Collins, and James Haug for selecting this book for the Juniper Prize, and to the University of Massachusetts Press for publishing it. My largest debt of gratitude goes to my mother, Sybil Pugh; to the memory of my father, Walter Pugh; and to my husband, Rick DelVisco.

Stardust Media

MY TWENTY-FIRST CENTURY

It started with Flaubert and a book about nothing.
Actually, it started with no books at all. Or no books
Of mine, at least: my book was only a germ inside.
It started with a turn at Butterfly World, with a swallowtail
Lighting on a man's brown shirt—its wings chafing
And lowering, paper-like. The century spoke in sopranos
Of every stripe, in chimes from Galaxy and Outlook.
After a decade passed and my father died, I would see
My first *Madama Butterfly*. When the towers blazed,
I'd stood on the shoreline, seared as I had ever
Been, and carefully watched that smoke cross the water.

SMARTPHONE INLET

Little ruby-diamond-violet inlay.
A jewel box streaming like the Russian
River etched among cypresses. Perspicuous
phones are what Freud would call a *reticule:*
a place to tap your fingers, or a sequin-
riven coin purse fragrant with enmity.
Must we reduce, until every embroidery
will fit inside the hand? Yes,
I think so. And maybe now you'll
follow me? Historically, women
would brood like robins on inchoate
letters pulled airily from cloth—they'd hold
hooped fabric at a decorous distance.
So soft words could never form
until they were needled. Afterwards,
the linens would read *Family*
or other chestnuts—*God we
Trust*. But those words were never
lit from within, the way that ours are.

AN ANCIENT TEXT

My dream was trying to tell me
something about texting.
Does our alphabet suffer
from scarcity now?
A man was carrying an *x*
into and out of the room,
half the symbol for a female
chromosome. The *x* was
on loan—like a painting
curated at the greatest expense,
then covered by crowds so
you hardly get a glimpse.
Then my dream turned its head
and asked me to commit
myself to hard-boiled elegance.
I answered: Am I elegant?
Saddle me. *And gather*
me / Into the artifice of eternity.
Funny, I've never
dreamed about a horse.
There's been so little
that I've wanted.

TOLL

I know you remember the clack of the keys,
but can you still hear the bell that rang in the paper,
several seconds before *flush-at-the-right-margin,* reminding
you to return the carriage, just as Cinderella did
at midnight? I don't want to make too much
of the bell. It took its place in the ambience of writing;
it rang for the typing pool and novelist alike. Still,
in those early days, every line tolled its own
unmelodic music. For me, it was the Eden of the sentence:
writing to people who could answer still. Writing to places
like Belclaire East, in Texas. A few years later, I could
type a little faster, and the bells followed true
on one another—sounding more like the machine
the thing really was, and less like what inspiration takes.

I DON'T KNOW HOW TO MAKE A WEBSITE,

even though I'm not *that* old. You might call me
ancient, but I still feel rather fly-by-night. I used to slip
notes under doors and scrawl my number in thick magic marker.
If you'd asked me then about a website, I might have echoed,
"Web-sight?" and tried to explain how the cobwebs in the boxwood
fogged dim shapes in the photographs I'd snapped with my
Instamatic camera. That was a lawn in which no leaf-vein was left
to chance, but I'd zoomed in on the exiguous pre-lettering
that sifted in the hedges to form points on a hypotenuse
I saw connect the bush and a filigreed porch column.
The webs razzle-dazzled me; my dad said they were "crappy."
That's a schism that persists today, when a lone cobweb
in a spotless condo's apt to furrow my brow: can this be
secret code? Or tiniest ecology? Missed-a-spot?
Knocking on Buddha's door? An *if* around design, that
white heal-all, keeps haloing the web-sight. It's hard to tell
if it matters or just clutters. But shoo-fly ambivalence
became the slope and snarl of my life—though I couldn't
have foreseen it then, not when the angel Gordon
Lightfoot sang *Cobwebs and dust,* with which he rhymed
I hate to leave you, but leave you I must. I still think
Gordon knew a thing or two about refrain.

VOICE ROAD

All the kids' bodies nestled their devices,
their screens as hushed as aquarium night-lights.
But that's not happening on Voice Road,
Michigan, which ends in a field cleared
by pirouetting tree trunks observed from a car.
Voice is the windlass that rescues diffidence
from splintering the everyday: *your* voice
sheltered me through sharing when I thought
I didn't want to speak. And many things
do happen in the wilds of northern Michigan.
A new young monk lofts Christ-like
in the monastery, floorboards kissing
his arms and legs and cheek. Now he's
risen, smiling at the Hegumen holding
his right hand. South of them, Petoskey
stones are acting much like hieroglyphs,
but short on verbiage no matter how you puzzle.
And Voice Road is always there. One clear
night in Arcadia, Michigan, I had a dream
about a dog named Missionary. Missionary
chased a ball into the river. Then *kicked*
at the constancy, the slower part of water
that my dream said resisted every tremor,
every arabesque. Then Heidegger, or Derrida,
asked me to dream of Van Gogh's shoes—
my husband's snowy Timberlands, kicked
out the door on the nights he sells Christmas trees

late into December. *Under the soles slides the loneliness
of the field path as evening falls,* wrote Heidegger.
And why should we chase a philosopher
from poems, if his words just lowered me, hand
over hand, to the loneliness of work?

WITH A SONG

There's something about music: the wish to
be in the dark. Like *I don't know what person
this voice must belong to.* At times I love
a secret, what sheers away from intellect.
Intrepid horn of birdsong when you won't
see or know the bird. Or sometimes
I'm riding in the car on I-80, dipping
my eyes into the glamour of Ohio, its red
barns or white barns severally unpainted
by tactile fingers of winter weather.
White barns with green roofs. Sky-blue
with white roofs. Wait, isn't sky-blue brighter
than any sky you really see? *Canned sky,*
you might reply, *hyperbole of color.* Platonist
Crayola blue. Would anyone trade a teal
feather for a trill? The highway will line
with mud and snow stripes along a fence,
then apple orchards spider in the ice.
A long stand of pines before the strip mall.
And still from the radio, an alto atremble:
I love not knowing who it belongs to.

LIKE TRUFFLES. LIKE CHANNEL-SURFING.

I love a word that melts in the mouth of my language.
Like *Truffaut,* or better: *tartuffo* in Italian.

I love lying back as the opening credits
are slowly chased into the distance
by faces.

I love the promiscuity of television—
its screen, I mean, since it flickers to anyone.

I love climatology more than the plot.

I love the bluebells on *Broadchurch,*
the ones I misidentified as lupine.
I loved the surveillance monitors on *Homeland.*

I love a refulgent Cornell box—with an owl,
a Pavlova tutu, a telescope. How I love a magpie!
I love a box whose EKG is Blu-ray.

I love that remote control is affordable.
I love the nuns on the three-hundredth channel
and their midnight campfire of

Holy Mary, mother of God, pray for our sins,
Now and at the hour of our death, Amen.

The sweetest drag of a D'Anjou pear-skin.
The truffle's salt, or its 80% dark.

I love my life in a nautilus shell.

HOT OR COOL MEDIA

I would vote for *cool* in the case of the color TV
my father built in 1970, with a white-silver knob you needed
all five of your fingers to pull, its edges as serrated
as a new quarter corn-fed. You'd have to plan your viewing
at least five minutes in advance, so the picture could "warm up"
from grey Zen stone to pathless stripes of *Via lactea*
to the dresses and slacks and polyester
faces of persons finally wired for sound somewhere
within those cathodes. In an interview once, I recall, my artist friend
seemed to speak of media as weather: said painting was warm,
not cool like video—a word not yet invented, I gather,
the nights I sat too close to the screen, hoping the Milky Way
cohered in time for the theme song set to tinkle
reliably at 8:00. She also named a painting "Touching
Everything, *for Alan*," which co-stars a square
rumple of red satin sheets, then corners
of some satin blue—two zooms, one
room, two saturated hues: yes, I can touch
what she makes me see; and just when it tells me its fever,
I'll realize she's right—that now I have no business
with chiasmus, that I won't exchange the one term for the other,
as happens far too often in the hopscotch of the sonnet.
The TV's cool, even white-hot plasma; and when dust
swirls on this laptop screen, I'll need a constellation map—
preferably with holes—if I still want to read.

TRANSPARENT

Some days the credits are more glorious than the show itself.
The rustling piano arpeggios: the font. The known electronic
initiation ritual. There seems to me some risk in a decorated
supplement—sky-blue rectangular eyeglass frames, let's say.
In contrast to such brightness, the framed eye begins to murk.
Enframement, for Heidegger, could mean too much ordering.
Anyway, the credits roll, ushering you to the show you know.
Opening the plot's current door: #3. But the credits don't
roll, these days. They'll have to smoke and star, like a TV
show's unconscious. Or we could say instead, *like neural
cartography.* So now assemble all your pillows. Settle down
and watch. How many times did I see stardust glittering
this girl's lips and eyes as she pressed her face to God?
A startlingly crooked tooth, every time she cracks the smile.
A face like a fresco in the corner of a transept.
Or the face itself is stardust, on the cusp of crossing over.

STARDUST MEDIA

*You know all the transcendent sounds. It's all sound all
the way through.*

—ELIZABETH FRASER OF
THE COCTEAU TWINS

Scat-track and yodel. A tone in cat's-eye marble:
then opaline filaments of vowel packed in ice . . .
this was how the Cocteau Twins measured out
their idiom. They named that album *Treasure*
like a dead hieroglyphic, and I recall its cover
as ersatz Hellenic—a half-shattered Venus
in a sea-glazed cloud. Am I right? Am I
accurate? I really want to ask this of my memory,
not the Internet. I want my mind to laminate
an image on the sounds I want to hear.
Maybe the historical rightness doesn't matter.
Or maybe my mistaking is the beauty entire.
In any case, I always thought the Twins
had voiced the Sirens. One of my friends
said, *You have to buy this! I've never heard
anything more beautiful in my life.* At the time,
I was admiring her taste and black hair.
So how could it be easier to lash myself
to the mast? *Like honey twining / from her throat
and my throat, / Who lies a-pining?* That's Homer,
but the Twins knew the Sirens would have
never sung in words—so their semitones
unspooled the way that bodies pool and crash
together, raptured after sex. Have you heard
searchers found debris from the plane

that vanished two years ago? I was reading
the headline when I thought I saw a stone
arrow pulled from beneath the ocean floor.
My mind's eye transformed it to the Venus's
hand, a triangular push of form interrupted.
And then I heard a Cocteau Twin
moving smoothest marbles in her mouth.

ORIGINS OF THE COLLECTION

From one stone came a collection of stones—
oblong planets with their own moons and
sunspots. Some were freckled, running
Saturn's rings around in mottled blacks
and pinkish gray. But before all that
came the first stone in shocking white—
like tibia bones, but whiter than I'd ever
guessed a skeleton could be. How clean,
then, is my own? Could it glow like
radium in the dark? Maybe Moby
Dick was a skeleton turned inside-out.
But this stone's a tranquil whale that
musters no resistance if you pick it up.
Stroke it, and your hand's on much
too smooth of a ride. No blowhole.
No lingua. No franchise. Just fluted
astro-stillness never muddied by a lichen.
Everything maculate abandoned
at the watermark. Blankness yearning
for the company of crowds.

MY HAND TOO BRIGHT A NIGHT-LIGHT

or the flank of an albino hare, scooting up the edge of this bullate
begonia leaf. About to nibble there. Not the shadow-rabbit
you'd coax from your fingers in a spotlight. It's more
akin to Stevens's barque of phosphor, little boat—
but *phosphorescent* seems too lyrical a label. I might try
bioluminescence instead: that trend beneath the ghosting ocean.
Fish emitting gas-light. Or ripples carve them over-white:
the scourge of a color that bleached Western history.
My hand's surrendering to that callow night.

EIGHTY PERCENT OF LIGHT IN SPACE IS MISSING, SCIENTISTS SAY

> *If we count up the known sources of ultraviolet ionizing*
> *photons, we come up five times too short. We are missing*
> *80 percent of the ionizing photons.*
>
> —BENJAMIN OPPENHEIMER,
> CENTER FOR ASTROPHYSICS,
> UNIVERSITY OF COLORADO, BOULDER

How bright, then, should the sky's mantle be?
How much more starriness could shake away like salt?
That shawl you're sewing: it needs another sequin.
Maybe we should make a trip to Vega Fabrics and
pick one out. That sun that knifed a quadrant or a sliver
of my cheek during walks in green Virginia? It's only
a fraction of what's missing. Some light is like Antigone,
embalmed in a cave sealed by rocks. But an artist's
studio conducts its own tincture of mercurial overcast:
look, there are bruised, flinty planets on the wall.
Gently, they'll generate a reading lamp from within
themselves, by which I'll re-read *Walt Whitman,*
a kosmos, of Manhattan the son.

Did Midtown squirrel away the light? Maybe it
swam beneath our laptop and iPhone screens.
Or we scavenged it with pincers from an unknown,
stillborn, ravishing technology. Whatever the cause,
there's *a deficit of ultraviolet light in the cosmic budget.*
So light can't balance its own bank account.
Or astronomers reach even further for metaphor,
accusing "tendriled" hydrogen of under-production—

as if a kudzu vine took too many smoking breaks
while riveting auto parts on the factory floor.
I've long sensed brightness is nothing but economy,

much as they also say capital's a figment of our smooth-
muscled imagination. *Gothique flamboyant,* the Notre
Dame tour guide said: the Gothic, in flames.
The psychedelic cypress in Van Gogh's *Starry Night.*
But capital's a wash when the gold standard's gone.
So swipe your card. Slip 'n slide. Our galaxy's
effulgence is malnourished, and nobody
quite knows why. The scientists' numbers
were four hundred percent wrong. Whitman
would have said, *Seriously? You're surprised?*
Frost would have junked the telescope.
Me, I'll settle in to watch this goldfinch
sock away a decent chunk of change.

A BENEFIT

It's back, the virtual. Not that it ever
really went away. I remember the word
stayed lucent inside me like a rainbow
in gasoline. Now I'm watching people
spinning slowly around—with cardboard
viewers pressed against their eyes,
their faces tracing spirals in the near
atmosphere. I think I see a fontanel
re-emerge under someone's hair.
In the nineteen-fifties, people
sat in cinemas and stared due north
beneath their 3-D glasses . . .
but in virtual reality, you have to
look *everywhere*. It wants you
to grasp that earth is a sphere—
and, wonderfully, your body, too:
your fingers so Copernican!
You'll feel this way as you
row the boat in Kenya, or jump
from a helicopter onto Paris streets.
Your newly softened ribs
will be cushioning your fall,
ironing out your every fear those
bones could be delicate on impact.
Or we might watch celebrities
ascend to clothe a vanished
constellation in New York. *It's
easy*, their limbs float lovingly

to those below. Light pollution
took the actual stars—but gods
still glide across the skinniest of
human forms: Poseidon glows
within the actress Rooney Mara.

PINK, PINK, PINK

Our fingers may not feel it when they're daubing
at our screens, but the West is always soaring
toward its own disintegration. Think of the Elgin
ruins or the star-chalk. The leggy Ozymandias?
Too obvious a metaphor. The Sistine Chapel's indices
are much more poignant. Adam's finger pricks you
when it grazes at the air: God so impossibly
near and far away—God so *figurative*! I'm talking
about art now, not the crescent billowing
of figurative language. I also need to water
a deceptively discreet horn sprouting sea green
from an undone orchid. Last night, we heard an Iowan
sing *La vie en rose* with, to my ear, no American accent.
And I was listening hard for a caving of the *r*.
Rose spotlights lit her. At first I was thinking—
breast cancer awareness month? Pink, pink,
pink, pink: skyscrapers' evening gowns,
loved when we're out on LSD (that's Lake
Shore Drive), their glass sashes colored by
whatever the monthly cause. When she sang,
I hadn't heard about the murders in France
or seen our own monuments lit blue, white,
red and American ambidextrous. But nobody
says *rose-colored glasses* anymore. That song's
become an elegy for slumbering dead metaphor—
or now, for 129 dead. Once someone told me
I'd built a wall between myself and the world.
Someone else said that I "always turned
away," to insult me. That's probably
true, but I'd rather call it *swerve*.

TIMBALE

The gluten's back. And it's pissed, a cartoon said.
OK, but I still need my gluten-free fantasy.
Scanning an old *Larousse Gastronomique*, I found
a photo portrait of *timbale Élysée*, a dessert that resembles
a domed screen fitted over green-spiked heavyish
cream, like Hagia Sophia latticing above your plate—
timbale, from the Arabic for *drum.* The tenderest
drum ever, with its "spun-sugar cage"; but it also
reminds me of James Turrell's windowed, slender
amplitude in caves. A quick pour of photons.
More of a slurp, really. "Centralized focus,"
as the art critics say—the aspect so much
prettier than the name. But back to the timbale,
please: what is this crumpled, vaguely
blossomed thing on top? It looks unfinished.
As if someone scrapped the calculus equation
that deduces the height at which dessert
should be scaffolded. Calculus does
have equations, right? It's supposed to build bridges?
I remember nothing from my high school class.
Except derivatives—who, when they wore their
diamond-emerald Tiffany rings, delicately
crashed the 2008 economy. *Corporations
are people, my friend,* Mitt Romney would go on
to say. Then his friends told us: *Here, eat this.*

OFF THE WEB

A dash of cayenne, or a soupçon of cocoa.
How is such a measurement translated
into time spent? If I stay on the Web
much longer than that, I'll feel my dress
gather headwinds and swirl, then lift like
Marilyn's over a grate. Or I'll find myself
in a hoop skirt stitched with undulating factoids,
like Lesley Dill's lettered dresses printed
up with stanzas from Dickinson's fascicles.
But I don't want to wear information!
It doesn't look good on me. I'm having
trouble walking in it. I forgot my sunblock.
Soon my face will burn in this electronic
shimmer—like the writer who lives her whole
life in the dark because every light source,
no matter how dim, will scorch away
her skin. She can't turn on TV or even
look through a window. And she may have
caught this affliction from her laptop.
It seems as if you'd find such an article
by accident, at midnight when you're
googling your symptom to the gooseneck
hinterlands of the Web, but no—it was on
the front page of the digital *New York Times*.
It's also a story you might tell yourself
to try to appreciate the things you still have . . .
how delectable is sunlight on your face
in early March? Medical science has its
own take on everything, but God!—
don't let my life be ruled by science.
Grant this wish, and I'll stay off the Web.

I'm Taking a Vacation on My Desktop

in my wallpaper of Pfeiffer Falls in Big Sur, California.
Do I need to explain that I'm referring to my desktop
on my laptop? Probably not, since *desktop* wouldn't conjure
up, in most people's minds, the astonishingly tiny square
of Dickinson's writing table—her *cherry* table, in Diana
Fuss's words, that really looks like a flat music stand.
You could only fit your score upon that stand—not five
dog-eared hodgepodge books, or patchwork hand-outs
with check marks. Her implements were minimal . . .
but wallpaper's something. Bishop changed it irrevocably
for me when she described the rosettes in the veteran
fish's gut—if you say *like wallpaper*, I'll hear Howlin'
Wolf wailing. Be that as it may: when I'm done or even
not yet done with this page, I'm going to revisit
the waterfall on my desktop. I like spots that appear
uninhabited, as this one did when we all crowded in
from the trail above—stretching our hands right
over the abyss so our cameras could fix something
person-less: blue-blue water; a white surf
swirling around rocks, etc. Do keep in mind
that my snapshot was really just a snapshot: nothing
either enhanced or shopped, so my desktop
conserves a slight vertigo of blur, which I also rather
like, since there's something stalwart about pixels
refusing to diet for a retinal display: I'm not
Gerhard Richter, but I'm sort of like a homespun,
talentless Monet. And when I visit Pfeiffer Falls
so many times a day, the talentless birds chirp fast
outside my window screen to gift some inaccurate
sound to the scene, since Midwest birds don't sing
the same as California birds. Even I know that.

But Shakespeare wouldn't care, and neither
should they. And the birds never sewed those
songs on a table, or even deferred them into
long-lost tracks of anachronistic shutter clicks.

IN THE DISTANT TWENTY-FIRST CENTURY

I was curled on the rug, re-reading *To Luck,*
the Merwin poem we'd framed inside our brick faux-fireplace,
when something drew my eye away from his lines
and into the glass that glazed the words within their frame.
What new reflection was jewelling my periphery? It looked
like a geometric magnet striped with gold and blues—
an inlaid mosaic!—or a modest altar retrofit with sapphire
and brass. I had to catch my breath, then felt a little
dazzle tracing down to my ankle. An altar in my living room!
An altar. To what? I told myself it didn't really matter,
then looked more deeply into the reflection, struck
by the patient *craft* of this thing: the gauzy imbrication,
yet fixity of its foils and shades. Blurred but somehow
lapidary. Blunted, yet opulent at the far left side
of Merwin's page. Finally, I broke the spell,
turned around, and scanned the room behind me—
to find my own desktop a-shimmer on my laptop,
sequined with Word files and folders
gleaming Byzantine, and dreaming in the half-glow
of infant daylight savings time: medieval little
rectangle I'd left and forgotten about for a minute,
reflected in the glass that shined the poem inside its frame.
So to live in a museum would be something
for another day. And W. S. Merwin? The unlikeliest
portal to the mirror of the distant twenty-first century.

*   *   *

THE CLOSE-UP

There's someone I know who hates small talk.
He's only interested in personal revelation—
what seems more meaningful than TV or the weather.
I was thinking about this as I sat in the theater.
From where I was sitting, I could barely glimpse
the conductor's wisp of baton and fingertips.
His snippet of hand was like confetti on the streets
of a city that celebrates an endless carnevale—
like daisy-shapes speckling Pan's alabaster hair.
And now, the sound from invisible instruments.
The orchestra buried. The ballet about to start
was *Romeo and Juliet*. I wondered how the dancers'
feelings would reach me without close-ups.
Then remembered being at a bar the night before—
seated so close to a woman that her face filled
my vast visual field: teeth, and eyes, and
the skin faintly mottled. We made small talk
and laughed before I realized: *Your face
is a landscape*. Like staring down a mountainside.
And still I felt the anguish of an intimacy
not consented to. When Romeo first lifted Juliet,
her feet pawed the air in a deliberative flutter.
Her movement changed the atmosphere.
I couldn't see the dancer's face, but love
grazed my heart across acres of open space.

AND MY BELOVED

A sentence fragment insists within the song.
Who knows why a song affixes to the mind's wall?
This one: it's a melody with a hammer. Or *satis,*
the enough. Our arms are enough. As they arrow
and open. Muscle like a white-gold bracelet
to unspool. The beauty of the body points outside
the body, as the dancer's arabesque says *look,*
look beyond me. If you think beauty cloisters,
you don't understand it yet: this is what
the accurately dancing body says. And what

the song knows. Three harmonic voices
will labor to express it. As does the violin
entering the steep lilied avenue, the catch—
its fuchsia infusing an erstwhile a cappella.
As the Song of Songs said the heartsick
were believers—love the church, love its
infinitely burnished sex. *My bowels were*
moved for him. The hole in the door.
How beautiful thy feet with shoes, my beloved.
And lovely your shadowed eyelids, my friend.

ALBA

That little slivered torch was like a lightning
strand, silver-white—flashing out beyond
the scrim my hair had formed against
my eyes, darkening my vision at the instant I
woke myself from several bureaucratic dreams:
that light was your iPod's light, incendiary
chord upon the plane of your nose and cheek,
rendering it momentary earthenware statuary.

NOVEMBER BEGINS

His skirt's Hellenic folds pleat a *stanza* on the stage,
whirling a beeline from torso to shoulder to the fingertips
that bead a dance in air. No centimeter shorn of nerve.
Nothing not electric. And I also saw a Cattleya orchid
past its day, shivering to sugar spun, with one petal lifting
its quizzical valediction. Ficus shadows silhouette
our yellow walls at night. Friday in the conservatory:
long fronds like Kodak paper bleached by sunspots—
nature dreaming of a near-extinct technology.
My crimson tree has combed itself of leaves,
cleaning the structure that can lattice a cloud.

FLIRT

The bank of cloud that night was like a smoother
lambswool, a fistful you'd pull to stuff
a pointe shoe for ballet class. Or maybe the cloud
bank was more like the tiny cotton coverlet
in a costume jewelry gift box—the rough-cut layer
you lift to reveal the ring. But rather than acting
inert like jewels, the stars began to flee right
under and over the opacity, conserving a certain
dialect of flirt—almost the way Haider Ackermann
draped some spider webbish filaments across his model's
face and then fastened them with safety pins
all along the girl's smoothly alternating thatches
of white and fuchsia hair. When photographed
from behind the scenes, the model looked
bushed, I have to say. But she passed
for a ghost orchid. A syrinx, with strings.
This was on Trocadero runway in Paris
circa 2015—after the super blood moon
made its last earthly visit until 2033. It was
not exactly bloody, but *La terre est bleue comme
une orange,* as Éluard would say. In this case,
skies were *black* as an orange, or a peach
moon harboring illegible, gray characters south
of the huge, pale, scrolled cotton cloud curl
when I sat beside my husband and my friend,
the three of us staring at the sky charade
with all our legs pressed against the white rocks
bordering Lake Michigan, and half our neighbors
there too, with telescopes and phones. Don't you

think the word *beside* says more about love
than almost anything else could? And safety pins?
They're ammonite fossils of punk bands, strewn
throughout the landscape in our thrilling,
torn debris. So I'll have to stay here
and make much ado. About everything.

HEADS UP

Try to resist the wetly obvious. To love the suffix
even more than the word it ends. The recessed
zipper, not the color of the coat itself . . . some might
call these things a *supplement*. To what we think
we're knowing. Like watching a dancer when she
rests after dancing, her surfaces drinking up
an image of branches projected on the front wall.
Her speaking hand's a canvas. The tree's less an image
than a place marker, really. It's a *screen saver*: figures
we might not forget before the real work starts.
The tree's lost its leaves but is fingering the sunlight.
The branches and sky now star the dancer's
arms and are staining her forehead as she
wrinkles it to speak. So light inflects her skin,
culling a strand of a scene she isn't watching.
This beauty? What we used to call *a breather.*

WHAT DOES THE CAMERA CATCH FROM THE WORLD?

Many things less glazed, perhaps. Sequins and skin quick-
draped to sequester radiance—at least if you're considering
my Canon with its one myopic eye. The world blinks right
when we're capturing its splendor: *Scappa!* someone called to me
last night: *escape!* Eighteenth-century painters tried to do
the same thing, but they were only catching at imagination's hem.
Just as the figure skater glides from a canon, launching from
the inside edge of his skate to land a triple axel without falling.
An arabesque in ballet's called a *spiral* in skating—that's odd,
since the lines of the pose are so straight. But in Ferrari's *Pan
and Syrinx*, the girl spins up into a reed like a twister. The reed
then becomes a flute, conducting the air as it hummingbirds
its way through. All to deflect a horny guy's advances . . .
but a chord of Syrinx's breast is ghostly as Mary's face
often is in mourning. That snatch of true religious, unmoored
from any ornament. Or from the port of health itself.
A saint like a helium balloon sorting skyward.
A saint like sunspots captured on a casement.
Or that epidermal diffidence we always think we see
embossing every "weird" kid remembered
from elementary school. Like me, as I was
and am. Something definitively not about the beach.
And look, Syrinx's eye is poking into darkness.
In botany, syringa means *lilac*, like the hedge
that bordered my swing-set in the old days.
When I swung, the lilacs' scent was a pendulum
anchoring, then lifting me every time my body
traced an arc against the sky. My teacher said
the odor of cut lilacs fills a household for days. Not
the *whole* house, my mother corrected when I told her.

HAVE YOU HEARD THE ANNUNCIATION?

Were you ever stunned by a police car's flashing lights? *This is
what will happen, no matter what you want.* In Bellini's version, the story
chafes like a wayward fly in the web Gabriel's robe has made: look,
the robe wants to say, the world will unravel now, whether
you consent or not. Then Mary's consternation cracks
open like a violin-case—but there are things she can't say
amid the noon voices of Western iconography. So highways
will furl, then triangulate the angel's hip. Or maybe you've been
blinded by a too-bright spotlight? In some prisons, *solitary*
means they never dim the lights. That might be akin
to the frequency of Mary's shock, crushed into the fabric
spangling faster than the angel's wings. *Thank God
things have changed!* we sometimes exclaim. These days
we write our own stories or, failing that, collaborate.
Our wombs belong to no one but ourselves, many women say.
But don't you get the feeling something's moving
your hand? That we're broken now by the genome,
if not by God? You're stirring dead letters in the Web's
silty bottom when you glimpse a mosaic of a long-
hushed history. Suddenly, your ancestor is sending up
a smoke-ring. And your eye is cut by a sliver of Gabriel,
whose hectic electrons could still shred your destiny.

BLUE ANGELS

After the pilot rockets to a nosedive,
the hillock of a contrail floats, swishing
someone's watercolor whitish
in the sky. An anorexic mountain—
or a precursor to cursive. Dietrich played
a blue angel once, didn't she? Or some
kind of angel? Last year in Charlottesville,
I walked the windy tarmac to my American
Eagle flight, then climbed the plane's
silver stairs "like 1960," I told my friend.
Of course, I wasn't alive that year,
but still nostalgia burned me—
or better yet, it *sheeted* me the way
it always does, as the Carpenters'
song from *Lovers and Other Strangers*
reminds me of my wedding day
before I was born. When I was young,
I couldn't understand Karen Carpenter's
voice—how a sound could be so
manly and quavery at once. Or how
two strangers became my parents.

THE WHEEL

The photographer Ghirri pinned the nametag *Azzurro*
to a monochromic sky's lapel, thereby snuffing clouds like
candles after dinner. Funny how a single word wrings nuance
from everything . . . he called his book of photographs
Kodachrome: impersonal, just as Mallarmé had cried, *Azure!*
Azure! in his hunger for evacuated Platonist chambers.
And blue is a color that insinuates behind so much,
like Giotto's busy frescos floating on an ocean.
When I was a baby, with color TV then in vogue,
a diet was a surfer's wave. And *Kodak* was the carousel
of family life, as the ad man Don Draper knew.
The wedding. The children: images that gather
a single tear within your eye. Then emblems
wheel, fanning the feelings to sell or quantify.

THE SHIRT

Charley Patton? The stranger stopped you,
pointing to the image on your old T-shirt.
It showed an intent man holding a guitar,
though his facial expression had been
poorly reproduced. Even so, the strings
seemed lonely. *I love the blues,* this stranger
was saying. *In Ireland, we love the blues.*
But in Belfast, not Dublin! Never in Dublin . . .
as for me, I'd had some trouble
deciphering the voices in old, scratched
recordings (as Patton's had been),
whether Irish or the Mississippi Delta.
They're really quite something, though, I found
myself thinking—these songs pressed
hard into the service of the body.
A song like a basket of sympathetic nerves.
A song that wants to train
the lungs in hard labor, spurring
their breathing like a riding crop.
When labor's your life, you don't
make an idol of the voice—
you use it. You'll make use of
anything to get you through the day.
Remember the ruby-wet comet
that girds the constellation
about to coalesce as a beige lace strip?
It was probably Vermeer's way
of lighting up the blindness
surely in store for the lacemaker

he painted, her patterns tinier than
8-point font. For years she'd needled
in almost-darkness. Fifteen hours
a day like that: first watering,
then floaters. A peripheral
coal spot . . . the eye can't remain
a microscope for long. It will turn
like a sunflower from discipline, mirroring
the pupil in a bright blood-blister.

PORTOFINO

Florid with industrial light, that lace store up the hill
and low above the harbor. The first wall was lace
strips made into bracelets—maybe a gift for the wrist
of my smallest friend. A cover of Dionne Warwick's
"Walk On By" was playing then, its English sounding
more like a cigarette's burning end. The lace was mostly
white, or light, with darker spears dotted in. *Fatto a mano,*
the proprietor told me; everything was made by hand.
He helped me with the bracelets' clasps, which I was
trying on for size. I'd recently visited a lace museum—
had seen a deer in torn brocade. And lace fish poised
in attenuated nets. By now, I knew lace to be
anything but frivolous—it patrols the very border
between craft-work and art. As a child, I'd failed
at needlepoint, but recently I'd seen I could fix
some points in air. Since many things I love are
strung with texture and resistance: a boat that lists
as it anchors in port. Or really any patterning
that anchors the whirlpool of what's intricate.
Thus lace bracelets counsel balance, living
on the skin with a roughness nearly palpable:
a feeling that transfers from an arm—inexplicably!—
all the way to the searching tongue. *Can I bathe
with it on?* my friend would ask, when I gave her one.

TRAGICOMIC

I love the lovely holograms in Jim Shaw's *Martian Portraits*.
Take, for example, this smiling man whose shirt reads *Kent*—
his head transforms to Martian if you're standing in the right place.
This change helps me realize how porous our skins really are . . .
how wispy my very identity. Last month, shopping for a mask
in Venice, I felt myself surrounded by a thousand plaster faces.
So difficult to choose just one! *Scegliere è difficile,*
I'd said to the shopkeeper, just before I lit upon a black
and gold half-moon mask with bars of music pasted on.
Allegro, it commanded—but the *g* had lost its tail
when the eye-hole was cut, since the staff was inlaid
right where eyeshadow stains a lid from lashes
to brow. In opera, they sing from the forehead,
at least? Of course I had to buy that mask.
Sometimes I'll remind myself: *allegro* means
fast in music, *happy* in an everyday Italian. But this
mask is sober. And the artist had signed *Tragicomica*
in back. When Hank was killed on *Breaking Bad,*
his brother-in-law Heisenberg scribbled his own
bald head into the mask of tragedy. His teeth
were soundless. His countenance—a thunderclap.
His mouth opened just enough to eat the universal
grief that's always nudging comedy, relinquishing
the paradox that steals its fluent way across
a face looking nothing if not human. *Or does it?*
I almost heard my moon-mask reply.

SCRIBBLE

Backed like a whale is what I might say, since Italian
graffiti always smears with a trace of the mammalian.
Nothing backhanded there. Nothing written anywhere
without marrow backing it, a scaffolding that reaches
out far behind the Renaissance and back to lapis-lazuli-
illuminated capitals, prehensile as the curled
hand depicted on a neighbor's frieze. I've recently
noticed that the oil from my fingertips condenses
to an oval near the center of my laptop mouse.
The stain is only visible in lamplight.
I don't make much impression on electronic media,
though some of them are smart enough to read
my very retinas, just to make sure I'm me.
I have no seal, it seems—and no familial mark
unless you count the illegible, monogrammed *P*
embroidered black on a black bathrobe my sister
once gave me. But outside: eye-bright echoing
on letters. A treble clef curls into sex-pink anatomy.
Morto ma vivo s'un supporto magnetico—and suddenly,
from the train: magnetism stirs your veins. Or skyish
ellipses, like a shimmering I saw the sun scribbling
away, shivering our curtains in the February afternoon.

ALLEGORIES

As I was tracking diatonic sunset frequencies
along the silver Ligurian Sea, with a camera ill-suited
to chase the veiled fibers or lacelike unveiling
of those diurnal vanishings—a Canon's retractable
lens, I mean—I remembered seeing Monet's first
painting from the 1874 show, and how rudimentary
I'd thought it to be: a discus shot from a fiery scrim,
dogging a slapdash figure in a fishing boat. Sunrise.
A big orange circle pasted up. Nothing too *plein air*
about it—more like a hothouse in the brain.
Was this more philosophical than haystacks built
in rose-sienna, gold or siltish in a chilly atmosphere?
Maybe. Before he painted haystacks, or chiseled
rough eyelets glazed with sun or stippled shade dotting
far across the Rouen façade, Monet was blunted
by the silhouettes of allegory. Why do they not go
breathing to the breathing world? Unlock the gate?
Turn their hidebound skins to the light? It might be
like an alien or star-born entity vamping the erstwhile
surface of the everyday: Scarlett Johansson in *Under
the Skin,* wearing sexy boots to murder her men-prey.
Lately, I've been scissoring magazine photographs
of roses and a brook at night. I could make a collage,
but I think I'll keep them flimsy. I never want
the sun if it's surveilling me, but bloom
like moonflowers whenever the light diffuses.
That's when I'll make my humble camera smooth

out some tides, or halt a palm shadow where there
rightly should be dappling. Every new discrepancy
between what I record and see will make me
feel again that counter-euphoria I always feel
when poorer instruments grace me with inaccuracy.

FROZEN MUSIC

Architecture is music in space, as it were a frozen music.
—FRIEDRICH WILHELM JOSEPH VON SCHELLING

Bach was a musical ecologist, the lutenist said—
from which I understand that, over time,
Bach conserved melodic scraps as ever-finer
glints in a greater coruscation. Think of these
persistent tunes as mineral sediment glittering
your fingertips—and shining over several days:
you've washed, but their stubborn stars remain.
For the lutenist, with antique strings, it all
requires listening ever more deeply to the
largish ear of his instrument, so his audience
will lean ever forward to catch the increasingly
quieter refrains of what might be an audible
cat's cradle. Spare as it is, such music enjoys
the recalcitrance of pigment: anachronistic
cochineal, hardscrabble indigoes—even rose
madder; though many people also tell me music
must unspool in time and thus encompass no
discrete space in the environment. But isn't this
where digital thought comes in? A video artist
thinks to harness an imaginary light incurred
by bow strokes or fingers pressing holes
in woodwind instruments, so every stray
vibration leaves a trace. Imagine him culling
skyrockets from sound: ephemera in motion
like the taillights and headlights on a freeway,
though ever more fleeting and less steeped

in teleology. Unless you count ascension
itself as a *telos*: his treetops are a moment's
growth, their leaves value-added like
lineaments of buildings half-inchoate
in an architect's plan. And now the projection
folds its drapery, costuming in frozen music:
trees form a steeple erected by chords before
a fresh wash of antique television static
will unnerve that view, undressing the image
in irradiated Belgian lace. Or undersea
fauna will gurgle, then bauble, to emerge as
Mount Rainer. If I remember right,
its foothills are named Paradise.

for Elliot Anderson

THE IMPERSONAL IS OUR PARADISE

The imperfect is our paradise.
—WALLACE STEVENS

Paradise is personal.
—*NEW YORK TIMES MAGAZINE* AD FOR NIZUC
RESORT AND SPA

It wouldn't be paradise without
representation: not in the civic sense,
but in the artistic one. So heaven's
never just a cloud—it's Whistler's
evanescence. And there'd be no paradise
without serious ornamentation:
take this leaning majolica vase, its
Delft-mosaic inlays and asymmetric
lip—and that almost imperceptible
wrinkle of porcelain, textured
like the shoreline ice that sheathes
Cape Cod in winter. Or this lava-
opal-rainbow ring with pinprick
diamonds studding its circumference,
its coloration muddied when the sun
muscles fast against your window.
It costs $12,000, the magazine says!
—but in paradise, you know
that ring would be free.
To anyone who wanted one.
Since beauty *is* beauty. Not just
the swindle of class or expense.
It's the eye ajar. Impervious. Aflame.

GLEAM

Consider the sashimi gloriously unsashed. The missing
sheath of it. The smallest sweep of it. The sunspot
arc of it. Madama Butterfly: the ladylike abject.
All that tenderness furiously unfiltered.
Like unrolled cigarettes: toxicity, with an aria.
Un bel di dappling the tongue. And somewhere,
a kimono is rippling with populace. With plains.
Ineffably. Or soundlessly: with trees.

THE IMPERSONAL

These urns are huddled in a dim conversation.
It's talk that I can't hear. One sustains the whoosh
of a god loped across it. A tigerish peony
striates another. But these aren't urns in
the usual sense—they're the backs of human torsos,
tattooed to show no skin-hue. No *skin* is really
what I mean: the epidermis cedes to a fiery
mural, as men tuck their heads to build
headlessness from behind our sight.
That wish to convex the ever-trailing body—
to make of it a pitcher pouring
anything you want. As Degas painted
a bathing woman turned away . . . her hair's
a slow fountain, her spine electrified
by the towel's rough pelt.

SHIRT NOISE

When I first heard the phrase, I knew I would have to
unearth a poem called *Room Tone* in a book whose cover
shows an open picture window. An ice-colored
trapezoid pours against the glass. A woman in a partial
state of undress was not what interested the painter,
clearly—though the hair against her ear nearly echoes
the malachite, floe-like field that the window opens
onto and loves. I trust this woman. She's a pillar
sustaining what the painter wants to see. That wash
of blue rectangle—it might be a curtain, might be a net
to capture rays within paint. And how rosy the arc
above the woman's left breast. The rose of sex,
I know—its faintest intaglio. This window is a journey
away from the human. And how I'll acquaint myself
with room tone. Every time we record our voices,
we're told to hold our breath for five long
seconds so the engineer can capture the silence
in the studio without any linen or cotton
or wool noise. What is the shape of that sound
I won't hear? The sere place our thinking rests upon?

THE STAIRCASE

A white jar dissolves into the whitish background
that gently presses its narrow form upright. Morandi's
ceramics must be manna for the eye, I think. Here,
their proximity makes several forms seem melded—
these jars with their wide or slender mouths. That palest
trellis of the air is nearly sexual, but only if you understand
sex is ephemeral as flowers: the scent of one jasmine
living only for an instant, but in the mind forever.
Like the ghost of the last jar I'm almost discerning
in this poignance of non-color. It's the highest
step on the staircase my eye must climb: a trap
door to nothingness. To sameness of aspect.
My feet are pressing interminable air . . . and if I fall
now, no one will be there to reach for me.
On my table, I've planted a candlestick in dirt.
Nothing's growing there but silvered form.
Or the mystic outline of a candle it used to hold.
I'll turn it around and around until it shows me
a new perspective on uselessness.

I CALLED THE VIDEO

The Steinway on the stage was so unusually shiny
you could watch the reflection of the pianist's hands
as he played a Bach chaconne. Within that mirror,
his hands were snowy hills that shifted in a winter sky,
but lambent all over like a longed-for bath. These images
presented as sound's near superscript—the numeral
that sweeps your eye low to the footnote
that finishes a page of information. Now I was
listening and watching, too, my seat on the diagonal
so I could see precisely the thing I called *the video*
his fingers had to feed. That quick cairn of wrists
before a stone toppled agilely from view.
A whelk, then the whitecaps gleaming it ashore.
His wedding ring also glazed at moments
while he played. Was I the only one who saw?
The only one poised to see? His hands' reflected
fury was the only sexiness to ascertain—
like a girl who whirls before a glass to find
the way a skirt will sculpt her moving legs in wind.
Or Balanchine's *Serenade*'s a song that hardens
dancers' arms aloft like trees: an arabesque
branches behind the orchestral note
like *instant replay,* rewound unto eternity.

*   *   *

LIVING UNDER A BRIDGE IN THE EARLY NINETIES

And I'm living off of grass
And the drippings from the ceiling
          —KURT COBAIN, "SOMETHING IN THE WAY"

I heard that at first, Kurt Cobain couldn't
get the recording right—until he lay down
on the floor with his guitar and just
murmured the words from somewhere
deep within his entrails. The lyrics are
talking about *having no skin,* as my new
friend concurs—no shelter from any storm:
a bridge's roof's not roof enough,
since how can a bridge even act like
itself, without walls? A bridge will
house the wind that blows within
a graven body. The body houses
the wind, with no walls. When Cobain
said that fish don't have any feelings,
I think what he really meant was,
Please, sir, can I have some more? . . .
more supra-skin barricade. Better
inoculation against flay. Is it true
when a fish bites a hook, it's like
a little landmine trips? The fish's pain
eats the sea. *Withindoors house the shocks,*
as Gerard Manley Hopkins wrote.
And men *rain against our much-thick and*
marsh air / Rich beams, he said, pressing
into verse the erections those muscle-

boys incited. I sometimes think Christ
is the *Oh shit* . . . in his poems: they're like
taking a vacation in a city draped in spathe
and fuchsia and cock and strobe-light—
then, *Whoops!* There's Christ again.
And maybe one day I'll hear my own
strange kindness loosen from its frame,
so new men and women will crowd
unto me until I'll call myself a wind
organ speaking its arrhythmic tones
near San Francisco Bay; or some
Aeolian harp being tinkered with
by trade winds' screws and faulty
copper wires—yes! Send me all your
freckles and spectacles, medicinal
twitches and your Carolina vowels—
friends, you know you'll let me
let you all love me. But soon
I'll have to leave those persons
in the distance and take a better
look at what's happening right
in front of me: a rabbit silhouetting
here is king of the goldenrod.

THE SOCIAL FABRIC

However slivered, however occluded, however brindled the light
you shined in your walks from building to building all these years,
over sidewalks forking the city, or across the violet harbor of the suburbs;
however vertigo'd my own vantage point—or myopic my ability
to see a lighthouse light its way through mist: I know that without you
there, something's missing. Or *lighthouse* is imperfect now, for what
    I mean—
none of us is a guiding light. We're more like an unseen planet's orb,
meaningful only when considered as a chip within a larger galaxy.
I mean chip as *chipware,* a table-setting broken but still serving.
Chips of shattered planet that emit a barely jangling light.
A whirlpool of jagged streams. Unthinkable necessity.
And how to feel my way into a metaphor that reaches
for exactly what I mean: our orbits always swayed by
even the most distant fragment in the pattern-wear: I feel it
beneath my forehead, just behind my eyes. This is why
I needed you, even though it's true we almost never had
occasion to speak. Because even the loneliest are never
truly singular: I'll always need what I almost never see.

for Brian Higgins, d. 2015

LINDEN

reads the violet sign on the train that began as a light
within the cloud-cover fuzzing the horizon-line—
like a shaft within a coal mine, or beams of research
streaming toward a raft of standing bodies: a light
now *Linden,* a Chicagoland suburban street named
for a tree, and the first word in a dialogue that two
TV police are having. One of them answers to
that leafy surname: pretty, atavistic, this auburn
detective who's delicately boyish with a ponytail
weightless as cumulous. But see—she's only
sometimes smart; she's barking at the wrong guy,
she's not even a decent mother, hugging herself
tighter as she wriggles in bureaucracy to dredge
the crap from a teen's murder (cut-glass butterflies
and stuff). But Linden loves that murdered girl.
And so we'll gather that she's "into" the dead;
she just likes them more than the living. More
than her own son . . . *weird.* But how weird,
really, when the dearest living snuff themselves
across the years, their wicks more compelling
than any boring flame? How would you even
know if you'd crossed over? *The water is wide,*
and I'm lowering my crazy body deeper in the boat.
My limbs are vegetation; I'll have to watch them
list against the current. And I can't stop watching her
making a career of it. Or maybe just a job. Necrolatry:
the beauty. *Linden* with her ponytail articulate

as foliage in autumn. The rain is falling gently
on Seattle PD, and a paper bud steams into a daffodil:
my house is a shroud. My window is its seam.

The Killing, AMC TV

PARABLE

I had no place to go. And no place
to spend that night of daylight.

Imagine my relief when you
offered your bed to me . . .
and knew myself forgiven

in your arms. My joy—
was it visible? Most of my life
I've searched for that forgiveness,
a state I seem to regard

as rest. This dream was
the tincture of Iñárritu's
Biutiful, in which a man enters

his last days on earth.
With all the razed buildings
and the gray. And all his loves
there, imperfect and delicate.

Soon he meets his young,
dead father in the snow, like
a horseman hundreds
of years old.

His father younger than he
is now. How I want to look—

but I can't look again.
Biutiful is how his child
spelled the word
that wants us in the world.

CARMINE LAKE

was the red well of Van Gogh's wishes
for his three bedroom paintings.
He wanted lilac walls and doors.
And got them—when he cut
this pigment with others,
before it burned out across
the unlived centuries, its brightness
dispersing like clouds over time.
When conservators show
their recent radiography, dark
pink particles will star
throughout the blue
paint's epidermal layers.
That's all that's left now—
the color's afterlife;
a certain loss of feeling,
like the darkness that fades
from our hair as we age.
Though I could be mistaken.
The first time I ever heard
my father cry (this was
on the telephone),
he was almost eighty.
I'm sorry, he said. *I'm more
emotional than I used to be.*

"*DEATH TO AMERICA* CHANT DOESN'T REALLY MEAN DEATH TO AMERICA,"

or so the screen told us; but a flag furl presently
switch-bladed into flame on the television's
wildfire diagonal plane, where an effigy
rippled Obama's face, his smile too big like—
oh—forty years ago, Carter's from Plains.
The other day I saw William Eggleston's
Plains photos: oak leaves and salt shakers,
blue gingham tablecloths—sentinel things
unsnared by any rhetoric that floated, jetsam-
flotsam, in the 1976 presidential election.
Eggleston liked the secret life of objects.
But objects are coy. Did they listen to politics?
Possibly, but all they heard were sentence
sounds flurrying fast over Georgia. The truth
was, they didn't vote. The truth *really* is
that I saw the TV in an oncologist's waiting room.
I was sitting with the healthiest-looking
person in the place, who happened to be
my father, who had come for his routine
IV-IG infusion—and who was, as it
turned out, closer to death then than anyone
could have guessed. The sicker people there
might have died soon after, too—or maybe
they worsened and, against all odds, recovered:
put their clothes back on, learned to sit
upright in wheelchairs, then re-take their first
gloried, staggering steps. Yeah—you better
believe that's glory, since my dad finally rode

in an ambulance to Hospice, in his hospital
gown, and he'd never wear his own clothes again.
But on that other day, in waiting-room
oncology, when no one could have guessed
who was the patient, him or me, and the flag
was absorbed in its slow burn on TV—he began
to look around him with concern and murmured,
People here look pretty bad, don't they. My empathy
was roused. I considered a patient in a surgical
mask and bonnet. She was watching the fire
with a certain kind of rapture. It reminded her
of a book she'd read called *Politics and Anger.*
Could she recall its contents? Where did anger
reside in the populace that scattered over France
before Vichy? Her mind was a kaleidoscope.
It half-filled with sky-blue glass-cut blossoming,
then labored to crystallize the book cover's
painting: three men in striped suits, juggling
three balls. Prisoners? A sorry little smidgen
of a dance? Or *Dying into a dance / An agony of trance* . . .
I was trying to inhabit her, one image at a time,
descending a ladder in the deep end of a pool,
and I saw the pool was only growing deeper.
And wondered, is this ethical? And then silently
asked my father, *Can't you see that you're the exception?*
Don't you know you're going to live forever?

STARDUST MEDIA II

Their bodies paused within a fountain of grieving,
four marble mourners in the Appiani tomb,
their robes poured out like ripples in that spring.
A marble corpse is prone. The mourners form a triangle.
One hides her face, as if to pray to Mecca.
Her hair sweeps the ground in a silent hysteria.
Hand to hand, the living will feel their way
to standing. But they'll have to leave
the dead man alone in the earth.

Joy Division's music was Manchester-gray-hot-pink—
Ian Curtis singing to his private epileptic stars,
bargaining with auras before his thrashing
fish could flip. The music itself was always
before: a baritone in quicksand super-electronic.
Dressed by euphoria in violin strings.
The dervish of his arms onstage, conserved
in YouTube archives, is now titled *epilepsy dance.*

When you don't want to live long, you sometimes
have to go with that. *Go with the flow,* they say;
do it with *grand mal.* When Ian Curtis first saw
an epileptic hit the ground, he reached for
a magnetic field from far within that foaming.
He felt his own heartbeat tremoring within her.
Then knew what he himself would do.
Scorch the stage. Crack his head
on a bathroom sink. Cut his own tongue out

when he seized. Or place a stone inside
the music: four marble mourners on the band's

last album sleeve. Christ's dead body robed
for the grave, dreaming of fugue and a welcoming sea.
In the Staglieno cemetery, Curtis's suicide threads
a marble daisy chain. With *Joy Division* scrawled
so fresh on the wall. And someone called Camilla
wrote her name there in February, 2016.

INSTRUCTIONS TO A DANCER

Pare to nearly nothing the movement
of the wrist. Move in a way that keeps
movement at bay. The wrist like a leaf
barely tousled by wind. More like a fleet,
infinitesimal unsettle. The thinnest
almond sliver. Or the arc a sigh describes—
but only the tip of it, never an achieved
exhale. Nothing but the template
for a tremble. Try to keep revealing
how we open at tenterhooks: within
the wrist's a blue vein. A suicide's cut.
Humbling, how much force it takes.
Or when you help the very ill to lift
a cup to their lips, you're witnessing
a galaxy impose itself between the
mouth and fingertips. Long-distance
body, underfunded infrastructure.
Fleets anchored at the dock. The tar
surface needs repair. Trains
no longer running in the grove.

WITH AN ABYSS OF WARMTH IN MY HEART

Gram Parsons's *GP* is rapidly becoming
an album I can no longer listen to, like many songs
sung by the Scottish singer Archie Fisher. Just last night,
when my husband played Gram's "New Soft Shoe"
at bedtime, and Emmylou Harris's harmonies were
twining like some rarest species of ivy over Parsons's
near melody, I wondered if my grief would ever
let me sleep again—probably you've felt this, too:
the coldness that kindles in the shoulder and then
travels down the thigh until the intellect
fails and then *you won't let me go.* A soft shoe?
I don't care about the words. It's the saddest
country tune that was ever written about
snake oil, or hawking house-slippers on what now
would be the Home Shopping Network . . .
that misfit between lyrics and melody, the strafe
and dissonance in irony. But irony's a dream-catch:
it's *fire i' the flint.* The way that Henry Vaughan
saw a boulder blazed from heaven that he hoped
would, in his own words, "kindle my cold love"—
since poetry's the only cure for girlfriends in a coma.
God's girlfriends, that's what I mean—as Early Modern
poets must have felt themselves to be. But if you're
looking for Parsons and Emmylou on YouTube,
try to find a certain grainy black-and-white take
that starts to dissolve their persons from the stage—
their skins and hair become atoms, deep abstraction.
Try to find the moment when Gram's shirt pulses, filling
the screen like an early fetal ultrasound, courtesy of

amateur Super-8 filming circa 1973. Just for an instant,
he's featureless matter—but then he's himself
again, troubling and beautiful and soon dead
from an overdose, his corpse torched at Joshua Tree
and then transported to the city of New Orleans.
There's so much I still don't understand about elegy—
how Parsons and Emmylou could sing as if his
dying were done then, marooned in the mournful
twang of their youth, so their every dearly-wrought
note burnished this imperative: *Preserve the sadness
of my sound forever.* Then even Henry Vaughan
could hear *the music of her tears.*

THE PARTNER

Steely Dan: Walter Becker and Donald Fagen

Among artists, for transport, we need to float
in medias res. Take, for example, the *two
persons with one brain* delicately poised
at the mixing bar in the sound studio:
see if you can catch the tail-end
of one's rumination on a bass chord,
the other chasing inspiration strung
on ghostly quarter-notes of velvet-
pineal jazz fusion. *I really like jazz,*
one of them explains. His partner
will answer with a shiver, with a stare
elsewhere, with a gentle chain of revived
syntax looping doubled cochlea like
battered tin cans across their decades
of listening or—better yet—of knowing
before listening. How would it feel
to never feel alone, to feel your thoughts
so permeable . . . to spend only your
waking with *the right one?* When they
made *Aja*, they mirrored each other
with a lick of alphabet, embellishing
*the quiet one might have with a beautiful
woman.* But they also knew the right one
is always a spire in back of the mind—
never the gorgeous body in your bed.

TO THE COMPOSERS

What I envied about you? Your hours spent
listening to the underside of old poems,
all for the task of setting them to music.
The iron-sides. The proto-howl: that this
was your *job.* That you allowed what melody
was buried there to float above the steppes
within the words. That for you, the thing
I love most—the filigreed or serifed thing—
remains what Michelangelo would rescue
from its not-yet-form. The chiseled poem
as uncarved stone! That in your quest
for music, you were listening for something
more: some wrong to make a right. And it
does take something else to see a finished
thing stay perennially unformed. A trap
door will open it. All of this reminds me
of Krzysztof Kieslowski's *Blue,* in which Juliette
Binoche finishes her killed husband's
unfinished symphony. Her musical staffs
swim dreamlike on the screen—in a ripple,
a scribble; then she chases them like
twisters in the landscape of that score.
Throughout the film, she'd had to bite
blue lollipops, mock-drown herself, and so on,
to get to the place where this was possible.
We learn that grief is a symphony and
can be completed. When I was younger
and alone, this film meant the world to me.
Now I know nothing really works

that way. I see that death's not lyric,
but that lyric might be one way the living
can survive it—oh, far from a guarantee.
Still, I'm thinking we have to utter
something in response to life stopping
stone-cold. How I kept trying to feel
his stopped pulse, as if somehow
I'd will it back. How to keep knowing
a lyric is rejoinder to the stone.

BUT THE AVANT-GARDE

did find ways to wear TV as clothing—the monitors,
I mean. Artists would steer a television's carapace
or stack one on two to build a flickering tower.
What have I learned from this? Machines can be diaphanous.
Or fleet as the Egyptian Queen that sailed down
the Charles River ferrying TV screens broadcasting
the waters they were floating on. An odalisque reclining
in electronic fire! But the best was the *TV Bra*
for Living Sculpture fronting Charlotte Moorman's breasts
when she played her cello solo, the bra's "cups"
actually two small TVs against her skin. Mellifluous
jellyfish agitated one screen, seeming to cast
their aspersions horizon-ward. Later, her husband
left a note on their car: *I have to park here, my wife*
has bone cancer, Thank you. She'd photographed her
scar when she returned from her mastectomy.
And closely crabbed a pain journal throbbing out
the instants of her terminal, young time. This was
a woman who swam through everything.
Who wanted to document every wilting thing.
And few of us feared radiation then.

A LUNG A GIRL

Chôbunsai Eishi, *The Poetess Shunzei no Musume*, from
the series *The Thirty-Six Immortal Women Poets*, 1801

Curated by the weight of her blown-glass fabric, the poet
is lifting her head like a cobra. All that billowed cloth
aerated like meringue. And hinged by her absent neck.
This is how a ship might coalesce from rhyming flesh.
Or possibly her horizontal body is a fish: her legs stream
behind her, rippled in the insects and half-done sepals
her kimono has imprinted as importunate waves. In a way,
this portrait reminds me of an iron lung: a head struck
from a silver tube. And how the tube curates a skull,
the iron whooshing rhythmically that breathing we know
is the last thing from lyric. A lung a girl could never leave.
She lay in it for decades. While a thing exhaled for her . . .
it's hard to explain. And though it looks industrial,
some patients felt the iron lung was soft as being buffeted
around by a summer breeze. Some had their hair fanned
outward, like solar rays. Others looked untouched
by the ravages of atmosphere. The wrong kind of love
discovers metaphors in this. And listens to my body
wracking only for him (for her): *The moon by which I once
finally saw you / now comes to rest in the teardrops on my sleeve,*
the poet-ship once wrote. Remember how Christina looked
in Wyeth's famous picture? Christina's pink,
shabby back enchanted by the black-belt open work.
Sitting her way up the hill. Magically, her swollen
fingers sharpen into tines. A girlish old warrior.
And thus, inexplicably, she'll serpentine.

NOW WHITHER FOR BRIGHTER COLORS?

Somewhere east of a retinal display.
Look inside a hothouse, where alocasia's
splashed its marbleized green on white,
echoing the skeins shading book covers
in Venice. Or look for alocasia that's
stemmed in magenta. Steamed to the neck.
Gold dust dracaena. *Cordyline fruticosa* blurred
in striations: pink and ecru. Pine. These are
the realer colors, I think. Are they brighter
than electric ones? I'm not convinced of that.
But I'm dazzled by a blast of scilla bruised
so blue on the roadside, especially
on rainy days. The wonder of that flower's
that there's nothing to compare it to.
Whither thou goest, I will go, is what Ruth
said to the one who would lead her.
Haven't you seen this with people
in love, or a new mother following
a baby with her eyes? The scilla's
hurting blue, I mean. Brighter
than my vein. Torched with violet
demi-grief, genetic in its pull.
To magnetize your restlessness:
not cobalt; not lapis. Not indigo.

WHITHER THOU GOEST

> *Where you go, I will go.*
> —DAVID LANG

I can't imagine lifting up a voice that didn't
sound like a pebble-ridden gully. Or just not seeing
the doubled-breasted consonants, three in a row,
that ruffle the ending of this poem's first sentence.
The song I'm hearing now has been combed
of every archaism: *whither thou goest* has become
where you go. Surprisingly, I don't miss the King
James aspirants that whistled in the older words—
the new vowels ripple to a stillwater impersonal.
And here I sit with strangers, our knees nearly
touching. From a window at stage rear,
a semi-transparent scrim illuminates the singers.
The stage set is afternoon lakefront in real time.
The skyline looks so small in the distance.
And the window makes a margin at the bottom
of the scrim, uncovering a greyhound's legs
and wheels on a wheelchair . . . all of them aloft
in the social world: it's April. But floating
here, near the bottom of this windowed lake—
I couldn't say if they move on sand or snow.
The conductor is conducting the canon
in his socks. His waist's long and curved,
with a dancer's density. All the singers' eyes
are following his hands—or *surrendering*,
I want to say, before my tears begin to fall.
This is how I taught myself to feel, I think—

witnessing somebody else's devotion.
After listening my whole life, I finally learned
my wedding vows. When I married you,
I repeated everything I was told to say.
I meant, *Where you die, I will die.*

INTEGRITY

How rapidly the Blue Ridge disappears—
and soon we'll be flying through a cloud
interior: *we're flying in the cloud*, I remember
she'd say, as the plane then entered what
nothingness would look like if it ever
had a look. That shredding of color . . .
long before *the cloud* became technology.
But now I'll have to leave these low
blue mountains, the ones that are never
ostentatiously sublime—just inward
shapes that soothe the peopled earth:
the farmhouses and trees I'll also lose
to our ascension, before I've lost
that last ocean-ridge above the grass,
the one that won't be asking anything
for itself. It offers a translucency,
always nearly mirroring the lower land
it also seems to shelter. Like a gifted
listener. . . . I guess it's still too easy
to ascribe such integrity to landscape.
But there's also some truth in it,
you have to admit. And look how
quickly, as if in self-chastening,
that listening must fade.

NOTE

Many italicized lines in *Stardust Media* are attributed to their sources in the bodies of the poems. Other italicized lines and phrases are borrowed from the following sources:

W. B. Yeats, Gordon Lightfoot, Walt Whitman, Benjamin Schwartzman, David Lang, the King James Bible, William Shakespeare, Giacomo Puccini, Charles Dickens, Gwendolyn Brooks, Henry Vaughan, Steely Dan, and Shunzei no Musume.

JUNIPER
JUNIPER PRIZE FOR POETRY

This volume is the forty-fifth recipient of the
Juniper Prize for Poetry, established in 1975 by the
University of Massachusetts Press in collaboration with
the UMass Amherst MFA program for Poets and Writers.
The prize is named in honor of the poet Robert Francis
(1901–1987), who for many years lived in Fort Juniper,
a tiny home of his own construction, in Amherst.